(2002)

Children
of the
ORPHAN TRAINS

Children
of the
ORPHAN TRAINS

Holly Littlefield

PICTURE
the
AMERICAN
PAST

Carolrhoda Books, Inc./Minneapolis

Front cover: A 1910 orphan train to Texas
Back cover: Ruth Hickok rode an orphan train to Iowa when she was five years old.
Page one: An unknown rider on the day of his orphan train's arrival in Missouri
Page two: These orphanage children are carefully dressed for their trip to new homes in 1918.
Opposite page: On their way to Texas in about 1909, boys face the unknown with a brave smile.

Text copyright © 2001 by Carolrhoda Books, Inc.

Carolrhoda Books, Inc.
A division of Lerner Publishing Group
241 First Avenue North
Minneapolis, MN 55401 U.S.A.

Website address: www.lernerbooks.com

LIBRARY OF CONGRESS CATALOGING-IN-PUBLICATION DATA

Littlefield, Holly, 1963–
    Children of the orphan trains / Holly Littlefield.
        p. cm. — (Picture the American past)
    Includes bibliographical references and index.
    Contents: Survival on the streets—From street to orphanage—Trains to new homes—Beginning again—Be an orphan train detective.
    ISBN 1-57505-466-3 (lib. bdg. : alk. paper)
        1. Orphan trains—History—Juvenile literature. 2. Orphans—United States—History—Juvenile literature. [1. Orphan trains. 2. Orphans.] I. Title. II. Series.
    HV985.L57   2001
    362.73'4'0973—dc21   00-009194

Manufactured in the United States of America
1 2 3 4 5 6 – JR – 06 05 04 03 02 01

CONTENTS

Above: For many poor families, home was a tiny room where eight, ten, or even more people ate and slept.
Opposite page: Children help their mother earn precious pennies by making decorations for hats.

Survival on the Streets

One day [our stepmother] said, "I won't give you darn kids anything to eat—get out and beg."
—Lena Weast, who rode an orphan train at age eleven

During the 1800s and early 1900s, millions of people came to the United States. Many traveled by boat to big cities on the East Coast like New York, Boston, and Philadelphia. They hoped to find freedom, jobs, and a brighter future in America. Most found misery instead. Their jobs paid only pennies a day. Even children worked long hours in dangerous factories. Finding food was a struggle.

New York City. Families with little money lived in neighborhoods packed with tenements, such as this street in the early 1900s.

Poor families often could not afford safe homes. They lived in dirty, crowded buildings called tenements. Children slept on floors or crammed together, five or six in one bed. The tenements had no bathrooms. They had little fresh air or water. Claretta Carman Miller's home had rats. "Many a night we woke up screaming because they ran over our beds and many times through our hair," she remembered.

Living in a tenement could be deadly. Diseases such as measles and smallpox killed thousands of people every year. When parents died, children became orphans. They often became homeless, too.

New York City. Illnesses and the need to work long hours kept many tenement parents away from their children. This girl baby-sits in 1890.

The Civil War also created thousands of orphans and homeless children. This war between the Northern and Southern states began in 1861 and ended in 1865. In that short time, over half a million men were killed. Many of those who died left behind orphans or wives and children with no way to earn a living. Often they lost their homes.

Gettysburg, Pennsylvania. This home for orphans was built after the Civil War.

New York City. Three children rest on a city street in the 1890s.

Children whose parents were still alive also became homeless. Sometimes parents were too poor or sick to take care of their children. Other children ran away from families who hurt them.

Life on the streets was hard. Children slept in outhouses, on steam grates, or in garbage bins. Most wore only rags for clothing. In the winter, they wrapped their feet in newspaper to keep them from freezing.

New York City. A newsboy prepares for a hard day of work selling newspapers.

Homeless children begged for food and money on street corners. Boys sometimes found work selling newspapers or shining shoes. They swept streets and ran errands. Girls collected rags from garbage cans, gathered coal, or sold flowers and matches.

To homeless children, the police were enemies. Many children had to steal to survive. Some became expert pickpockets. Others joined gangs. Children could also be arrested just for being homeless. Many who needed food and a safe home ended up in jail instead.

On the street, children learned to be tougher than their years.

Above: New York City. The Hebrew Orphan Asylum provided a home for Jewish children in need.
Opposite page: New York. Orphanage children enjoy a day of sledding in 1912.

FROM STREET TO ORPHANAGE

My father was killed and my mother died in 1918 of the flu.
[My brother and I] lived with people unknown, until . . . we
were taken to an orphanage.
—Alexander Douthit, who rode
an orphan train at age five

People began to worry about the many orphans and homeless children who lived on the streets. They built orphanages to give some of these children a place to live. But most orphanages welcomed only white children. African American and Asian American children were usually left to fend for themselves.

New York City. Children say their evening prayers at an orphanage called the Five Points House of Industry.

Orphanages had strict rules. The children had to wear uniforms. Each day was divided into time for meals, religious services, schoolwork, and chores. Children who broke rules were given extra chores—or worse. Helen Bailey Hayes lived in an orphanage in New York City when she was five. "One time they served rice. . . . I refused to eat it. For this, I was locked in a pantry," she wrote. Some rule breakers, especially boys, were beaten.

The orphanages wanted to teach children to support themselves. So the children were expected to work. Boys were taught trades like shoemaking or printing. Girls learned to sew, cook, and do laundry.

Girls learn to make hats at an orphanage in the early 1900s.

Life in an orphanage was almost always better than life on the streets. But orphanages were crowded. The food was usually terrible, and many children died from diseases. Younger children were sometimes beaten by older ones.

New York City. Children eat a free lunch given out by a charity.

Charles Loring Brace founded the Children's Aid Society in 1853.

Some people thought that orphanages were bad for children. Charles Loring Brace was in charge of the Children's Aid Society in New York City. This charity ran orphanages and schools for homeless children. Brace believed that children should be taken away from the dangers of city life.

In the 1850s, Charles Loring Brace asked families in the country to take poor city children into their homes. The families were expected to treat the children like their own. In exchange, the children would help with the farmwork and housework.

A boy learns to plow at the Brace Farm School, where children were taught how to do farm chores.

Worries and hopes show on the faces of a group of boys about to board a train to Kansas in 1904.

At first, children were sent to families in eastern states like New York and New Jersey. But there were not enough families in those states for all the children. In 1854, the Children's Aid Society began to send children on trains to states farther west. Other charities soon did the same. These trains came to be called orphan trains.

Above: Only the healthiest, strongest, and best-looking children were chosen to ride the orphan trains.
Opposite page: Boys prepare to leave for Texas in 1912.

TRAINS TO NEW HOMES

"We had no idea where we were going, just that we were off to find a MAMMA and a DADDY."
—Arthur Field Smith, who rode
an orphan train at age four

Not all homeless children went west. The charities chose carefully. Only children who would be welcomed into western towns were sent. White families there wanted healthy, hardworking white kids. Very few African American or Asian American children were put on the orphan trains.

Some orphan train riders really were orphans. But many were not. Children whose parents were too poor or sick to care for them were often sent on the trains. The parents usually were not told where their children were going. Most families never saw each other again.

Emma Toba and her brother, Herman, were abandoned by their mother in about 1916. They later traveled on an orphan train to Texas.

The four youngest children in this photograph were placed on an orphan train in 1916 by their older sister's husband, who did not want to care for them.

Many children did not understand that they were leaving forever. Claretta Carman Miller was eight when she went west. She remembered, "We had no idea where we were going, only that it was a long way and we would travel by train."

The children were carefully prepared to impress their new families. Their hair was washed and cut. They took baths. Girls wore new dresses and hair ribbons. Boys wore new neckties and jackets.

A well-dressed group prepares to go west in 1910.

Two agents brought these children to Iowa in 1906.

An adult always traveled with the children. The Children's Aid Society called these adults agents. It was the agents' job to see that the children arrived safely and found new homes.

Orphan train riders gather in front of—and on—the train that will carry them to a new life.

Once the children were ready, they were loaded into train cars, and their journey began. Children who had never left the city were amazed to see farms and forests. They were excited by the adventure of traveling to a new place. Lena Weast's train even stopped at Niagara Falls to see the amazing waterfall.

The trip wasn't all fun. The children usually slept on the floor or on hard wooden benches. Sometimes there wasn't enough food. Four-year-old Margaret Branden ate nothing but mustard and bread during her journey. The children were also scared about the future. Would their new families be kind? Would they like living on a farm? Would they find new friends?

Boys look toward an uncertain future on a train to Texas in 1910.

WANTED!
HOMES FOR CHILDREN

A company of homeless children from the East will arrive at LEBANON, MISSOURI, on

Thursday, December 30, '09

These children are of various ages and of both sexes, having been thrown friendless upon the world. They come under the auspices of the Children's Aid Society, of New York. These children are well disciplined, having come from the various orphanages. The citizens of this community are asked to assist the agent in finding good homes for them. Persons taking these children must be recommended by the local committee. They must treat the children in every way as members of the family, sending them to school, church, Sabbath school and properly clothe them until they are 18 years old. The following well known citizens have agreed to act as a local committee to aid agents in securing homes:

W. I. Wallace	J. W. Farris	J. G. Lingsweiler
E. B. Kellerman	Sam Farrar	Dr. J. M. Billings

Applications must be made to, and indorsed by, the local committee. An address will be given by the agent. Come and see the children and hear the address. Distribution will take place at the OPERA HOUSE, Thursday, December 30, at 10 a. m. and 2 p. m.

B. W. TICE, MISS A. L. HILL, Agents, 105 E. 22nd St., New York City
J. W. SWAN, University Place, Neb., Western Agent.

Above: A newspaper advertisement invites the residents of Lebanon, Missouri, to "Come and see the children."
Opposite page: Jean Sexton poses for a portrait with her foster mother in Missouri.

Beginning Again

*At every stop, we were all taken off the train and lined up for
inspection. . . . The people looked us all over, like cattle. Most
really only took us for how much work we could put out.*
      —Helen Bailey Hayes, who rode an
                  orphan train at the age of five

Some charities found homes for the children before sending them west. When these children arrived, their new families were waiting. But the Children's Aid Society had a different way. They placed notices in newspapers to tell people when an orphan train was coming. People who wanted a child could come and pick one out.

Most orphan trains stopped at several towns. When a train arrived, the agent would line the children up at a church, meeting hall, or school. Sometimes hundreds of curious people came to see them. Some wanted to find a child to love. Others were just looking for workers. The agents were supposed to place the children with caring families, but often almost anyone was allowed to take a child.

The children described in the advertisement on page 30 arrive in Missouri in 1909.

Chosen by different families, Howard and Fred Engert were separated after riding an orphan train to this site in Nebraska in 1925. They later reunited.

Most families were willing to take only one child. Brothers and sisters were often split up. In some cases, siblings were spread out over several states and never saw one another again. Other children found themselves living only a few miles away from their brothers or sisters.

Posters like this one were put up to encourage adults to visit children who had not yet been chosen.

Some children were not chosen. "I will never forget that Saturday," Robert Hemming Petersen remembered. "At the end of the day, no one had selected me." These children had to get back on the train and travel on to the next town. They worried that they would never find homes.

Some children were treated terribly by their new families. Ruth Hickok was chosen by an Iowa couple when she was five. "That night, I cried so hard that they locked me in the cellar where I sat in the dark, clung to the steps and cried some more," she remembered. Many orphan train riders found that a new home meant long hours of work and little food.

After suffering with the first family that chose her, Ruth Hickok was sent to "a wonderful home" on a farm.

Agents were supposed to visit all the children at least once a year. If any were being treated harshly, the agent would find them another family. But many agents did not have time to visit every child. Some children suffered for years with bad families. Others ran away. They worked, returned east, or tried to find kinder families.

Maurice de Leleu made the best of his work in his family's cotton field after riding an orphan train to Weatherford, Texas.

An orphan train brought the boy wearing glasses, whose name is not known, to a new family with three siblings.

The orphan trains did help some children find safe, loving homes. Willie Dunnaway was welcomed by a kind Arkansas couple who longed for a child. "I became the luckiest boy on earth," he wrote. "I was adopted by Charles W. Dunnaway and his wife, Maggie Dunnaway."

After taking an orphan train to Indiana, Andrew Burke served as a drummer boy in the Civil War. He later became the second governor of North Dakota.

Many orphan train riders grew up to be successful in their new communities. A few even became famous. John Brady was elected governor of Alaska. Another rider, Andrew Burke, became the governor of North Dakota.

By the 1920s, people had begun to change their minds about the orphan trains. The government started to work to help poor families stay together. The last orphan train left New York City in 1929.

In seventy-five years, the trains took more than 150,000 children to new homes. As adults, many orphan train riders have shared their stories with their own children and with others. They have helped to make sure that the orphan trains will never be forgotten.

These orphan train riders found homes—for better or worse—in Missouri in 1910.

Be an Orphan Train Detective

The orphan trains brought more than 150,000 children to forty-seven states. No matter where you live, it's likely that at least one orphan train came to your state or to one nearby. How many children did the trains bring to your area? What happened to them at the end of their journey? Is your community home to an orphan train rider or the descendants of a rider? (Since the last orphan trains went west more than seventy years ago, most of the children who rode the trains are no longer living. But historians believe that about five hundred orphan train riders are still alive. Many are eager to share their stories with their communities.)

It can be difficult to uncover information about the past. To learn about orphan trains in your area, you'll have to write letters and ask many questions, so you might want to ask classmates for help. Even working together, you may not find out all you want to know. But by becoming orphan train detectives, you could discover a forgotten piece of your community's history.

1. Look for mentions of your state in this book. Then read *The Orphan Trains* and *Orphan Train Rider*, listed on pages 45 and 46, and visit the websites listed on page 46. Take notes on what you learn.

2. Next, find out if your area has a state or local history museum or historical society. Look in the telephone book under "museum" and "historical society," or ask a teacher or librarian for help. Then write a letter to request information about the orphan trains in your area. Your letter might look something like this:

[your school's address]

[date]

Dear Historian:

Our class is learning about the orphan trains, which brought children from eastern cities to new homes between 1854 and 1929. We would like to find out whether any orphan trains came to our state. Do you have any information that might help us? We would especially like to know where the orphan trains stopped, how many children they brought, and whether any orphan train riders or their descendants live in our state.

We would be glad to write to another source if you have any suggestions. Thank you for any information you can provide.

Sincerely yours,
[your names]
[your teacher's name, your grade, and your school's name]

3. When you receive a reply, send a thank-you note to the person who wrote. Follow up on what you've learned so far. Does your city or town have a library that might have stored old newspapers from the time of the orphan trains? If you know the date and location of a train's visit, a librarian may be able to help you find an article about it. A librarian can also help you review current newspapers for articles about orphan train history.

4. You can also write to the Orphan Train Heritage Society of America, 614 East Emma Avenue, #115, Springdale, AR, 72764-4634. This organization records and preserves the history of the orphan trains. The OTHSA may know of riders or descendants of riders who live in your state.

5. If you discover that a rider or a rider's descendant lives near your school, invite that person to visit. You may have a chance to hear about the orphan trains from someone who experienced one personally. Ask permission to make a tape recording or video of your visitor's speech.

6. Share what you've learned. Write an article for your school newspaper or local newspaper, or create a presentation for a school website. Even if you haven't learned much about orphan trains in your state, you can still share this surprising part of American history with the rest of your community.

NOTE TO TEACHERS AND ADULTS

For children, the days of the orphan trains may seem like part of a distant past. But there are many ways to make the trains and their riders come alive. Along with helping children research the history of orphan trains in your state, you can explore America's orphan train past in other ways. One way is to read the books listed on pages 45 and 46. Another way to explore the past is to teach young readers to study historical photographs. Historical photographs hold many clues about how life was lived in earlier times.

Ask your children or students to look for the details and "read" all the information in each picture in this book. For example, how are poor, orphaned, and homeless children dressed in the photographs on pages 6 to 20? How are children dressed after being chosen to ride on an orphan train (pages 1, 2, 21–23, 26–29, and 32)?

To encourage young readers to read historical photographs, have them try these activities:

A Day in an Orphanage

Read the text and study the photographs on pages 15–20. Make a list of the activities children did each day in the orphanages described in this book. Put the activities in order, from morning to night. Next, make a list of the things you do each day, from morning to night. Include the time you spend at school, with friends, with your family, and doing chores. How are your lists alike? How are they different? How would your life be different if you lived in an orphanage at the time of the orphan trains?

Recording the Ride

Imagine that you are one of the orphan train riders pictured or quoted in this book. Read the text and study the photographs on pages 21–39. Then write a journal describing your experiences on your trip. Who have you left behind? Are you traveling with a sister or brother? What do you see on the way? Write about how you spend the long hours on the train and what you hope to find at the end of your journey. Include a description of stopping at a town where children line up to be chosen. Are some sent back onto the train? How about you?

First Meetings

Read the text on pages 31–37 and study the photographs of orphan train riders with the families who chose them. Next, imagine that you are an orphan train rider meeting your new family for the first time. Write a short play about this experience. Your cast of characters might include you, other orphan train riders, an agent, and the members of your new family. Begin your play at a meeting hall or church where you are chosen. What do you say to your new parents? What do they say to you? What happens when you go with them to your new home? Dress in costume and act out your play with children in your class.

RESOURCES ON THE ORPHAN TRAINS

Buchanan, Jane. *Gratefully Yours*. New York: Farrar, Straus & Giroux, 1997. After a fire kills her family, Hattie travels by orphan train to Nebraska, where she finds a home with a couple whose son has died. Hattie struggles throughout the novel to cope with the coldness of her foster parents, who show her no affection.

Bunting, Eve. Illustrated by Ronald Himler. *Train to Somewhere*. New York: Clarion, 1996. In this picture book, Marianne rides from stop to stop on an orphan train to Iowa. Plainer and weaker than the other children, she can only watch as they are chosen ahead of her. Will anyone want to bring her home?

Fry, Annette R. *The Orphan Trains*. New York: New Discovery Books, 1994. Illustrated with historical photographs, this volume describes the problems that led to the creation of the orphan trains, the experiences of children who rode them, and the reasons the orphan train programs ended.

Nixon, Joan Lowery. *David's Search*. New York: Delacorte Press, 1998. Part of the Orphan Train Children series, this novel tells the story of David, a child living on the streets of New York. David's life changes dramatically when he rides west to a farm in Missouri and befriends a former slave.

Tamar, Erika. *The Midnight Train Home*. New York: Knopf, 2000. Eleven-year-old Deirdre O'Rourke, the main character of Tamar's novel, is sent west with her brothers on an orphan train to escape their life in a tenement. Separated from her brothers and placed with an unkind couple, Deirdre must use her wits to find her way to a better life.

Warren, Andrea. *Orphan Train Rider: One Boy's True Story.* Boston: Houghton Mifflin, 1996. Warren tells the moving story of Lee Nailling, an orphan train rider whose journey began with abandonment, led to separation from his brothers, and ended with acceptance in a loving family.

Websites
<http://pda.republic.net/othsa/>
The official website of the Orphan Train Heritage Society of America is devoted to sharing the stories and preserving the memory of the orphan trains. The site includes interviews, photographs, and a reading list.

<http://www.hamilton.net/subscribers/hurd/index.html>
Howard Hurd, an orphan train rider whose photograph appears on page 33 of this book, shares his story through family photographs and provides links to other orphan train websites.

<http://www.pbs.org/wgbh/amex/orphan/index.html>
This website describes *The American Experience: The Orphan Trains,* a PBS television program about the trains. The site includes stories of orphan train riders, historical photographs, a transcript of the program, and a teacher's guide.

New Words

agent: an adult who brought children to new homes on a train

orphan: a child whose parents are no longer living

orphanage: a home for children whose parents cannot care for them or are no longer living

orphan train: a train that took homeless children to new homes across the country between 1854 and 1929

smallpox: a disease that causes fever, a rash, and often death

tenement: a building that is divided into many small apartments. Tenements are often dirty and overcrowded.

Index

TIME LINE

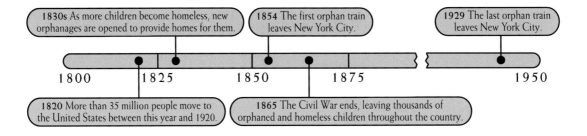

1830s As more children become homeless, new orphanages are opened to provide homes for them.

1854 The first orphan train leaves New York City.

1929 The last orphan train leaves New York City.

1800 · 1825 · 1850 · 1875 · 1950

1820 More than 35 million people move to the United States between this year and 1920.

1865 The Civil War ends, leaving thousands of orphaned and homeless children throughout the country.

ABOUT THE AUTHOR

Holly Littlefield has been a columnist, a waitress, a manuscript reader, a high school English teacher, and a volunteer counselor for runaway teens. She is currently teaching at the University of Minnesota. She lives in Minneapolis with her husband and two sons. In her eight books for children, she has written about topics such as Japan, Ghana, American pioneer children, and the Triangle Shirtwaist Company fire of 1911.

"After reading hundreds of orphan train riders' stories," she says, "I am amazed by these children's ability to survive and often remain positive despite the sad events of their lives."

ACKNOWLEDGMENTS

The publisher gratefully acknowledges the use of quotations from: Michael Patrick, Evelyn Sheets, and Evelyn Trickel, *We Are a Part of History: The Story of the Orphan Trains*. Santa Fe, NM: The Lightning Tree, 1990; Mary Ellen Johnson, compiler, *Orphan Train Riders: Their Own Stories*, vol. 2. Springdale, AR: Orphan Train Heritage Society of America, 1993. The photographs in this book appear courtesy of: © The Children's Aid Society, front cover, pp. 5, 8, 17, 18, 20, 21, 22, 26, 27, 29, 30, 34; © Ruth Hickok/permission granted by Jerry Hickok, back cover, p. 35; Courtesy of the Orphan Train Heritage Society of America, pp. 1, 37; © Bettmann/CORBIS, pp. 2, 6, 9, 11, 12, 13, 14, 19; © Library of Congress, neg. no. LC-H5-2709, p. 7; © U. S. Army Military History Institute, p. 10; © New York State Historical Association, Cooperstown, p. 15; © UPI/Bettmann-CORBIS, p. 16; Courtesy of Marcelle Hopper, pp. 23, 36; © Helen Hale Vaughn/permission granted by Orphan Train Heritage Society of America, p. 24; © John A. Mahey/permission granted by Orphan Train Heritage Society of America, p. 25; © The Kansas State Historical Society, Topeka, Kansas, p. 28; © Jean Sexton/permission granted by Clark Sexton, p. 31; © Kirk Pearce Collection, pp. 32, 39; permission granted by Howard Hurd, p. 33; © State Historical Society of North Dakota, p. 38.